Ugly CHRISTMAS SWEATER PARTY BOOK

The Definitive Guide to Getting Your Ugly On

Brian Miller, Adam Paulson, and **Kevin Wool**
aka Team Ugly of UglyChristmasSweaterParty.com

Abrams Image
New York

EDITOR: Jennifer Levesque
DESIGNER: Glenn Gontha at Gontha Design Studio
PRODUCTION MANAGER: Alison Gervais

Library of Congress Cataloging-in-Publication Data
Miller, Brian.
Ugly Christmas sweater party book : the definitive guide to getting your ugly on /
Brian Miller, Adam Paulson, and Kevin Wool, a.k.a. Team Ugly of UglyChristmasSweaterParty.com.
p. cm.
ISBN 978-0-8109-9752-3 (alk. paper)
1. Christmas—Humor. 2. Clothing and dress—Humor. I. Paulson, Adam. II. Wool, Kevin. III. Title.
PN6231.C36M55 2011
793.2'2—dc22

2010046228

Printed and bound in China
10 9 8 7 6 5 4 3 2 1

Abrams Image books are available at special discounts when purchased in quantity for premiums and promotions
as well as fundraising or educational use. Special editions can also be created to specification. For details, contact
specialsales@abramsbooks.com or the address below.

ABRAMS
THE ART OF BOOKS SINCE 1949

115 West 18th Street
New York, NY 10011
www.abramsbooks.com

CONTENTS

THE LEGEND AND LORE OF
the Ugly Christmas Sweater Party

Many subjects are often disputed across the landscape of this great nation. Issues relating to politics, foreign policies, and even athletics have been topics that have dominated many disputes. But recently a new argument has polarized the masses: Where was the first Ugly Christmas Sweater Party held?

Solid arguments have been made as to where and when this phenomenon was spawned. Folks in Kansas City have waved their BBQ-sauce—stained hands in protest as they are convinced that the idea originated there, while the fine citizens of San Francisco have spit out mouthfuls of Rice-A-Roni at the claims that the tradition started anywhere other than northern California. Countless students claim the first parties were thrown at their respective colleges or universities, and many families swear that their annual Christmas gatherings, whether accidentally or purposely, are the true birthplace of the parties.

In our quest to uncover the truth, our research has taken us far and wide. For well over forty-five minutes, we dug through dozens of periodicals, gossip magazines, and old photographs and came up empty-handed. We came to the conclusion that just as we will never know who invented the George Foreman Grill, we may never truly know who threw the first Ugly Christmas Sweater Party—but we have a pretty good idea of where it was held.

In 2001, while Americans were trying to figure out what to do with the surplus of food they stockpiled for the Y2K crisis that never was, our neighbors to the north were trying to figure out what to do with the surplus of Ugly Christmas Sweaters

there's actually a use for those Christmas sweaters that Grandma keeps buying you. It has since evolved into the world's premier stop for all things Ugly-Christmas-Sweater—related. Often imitated but never duplicated, www.UglyChristmasSweaterParty.com has become the foremost authority in the Ugly Christmas Sweater industry.

Over the years, we have acquired an abundance of Ugly Christmas Sweater Party knowledge. So we decided it was time to share our treasure map to happiness with you lucky folks who hold this guide in your hands, so that you can throw the best Ugly Christmas Sweater Party of all time.

that they had amassed since Canada was founded in 1867. It turns out some creative Canucks from Vancouver not only found an answer to their nation's most pressing issue, but started what has become the fastest-growing holiday tradition.

It has only been during the past few years that the popularity of Ugly Christmas Sweater Parties has taken off. The huge surge of interest has been attributed to the beginning of www.UglyChristmasSweaterParty.com in 2007. The website was started to get the word out that

CHAPTER 1

Make It Ugly

AND THEY
WILL COME

I BELIEVE
IN
Santa Claus

Ugly is the new black, so getting people to come to your party shouldn't be tough. We'll walk you through choosing which type of party to plan, when to schedule it, and how to get the word out.

PICK A PARTY, ANY PARTY

It's often said that variety is the spice of life, and Ugly Christmas Sweater Parties are no exception. Everywhere you look during the holidays, Ugly Christmas Sweater Parties seem to be, well, everywhere! People are turning charity events, office parties, family get-togethers, even pub crawls into Ugly Christmas Sweater Party extravaganzas. Your mission, should you choose to accept hosting duties, is to pick whichever type of party works best for you and your potential guests.

A Charity Event

The most popular form of Ugly Christmas Sweater Party is the charity fundraising event. Hosting a charity event is a great way to benefit your community, involve local businesses, and even get Too Cool Tracy (SEE CHAPTER 5) to don her ugliest sweater. The downside to this type of party is you'll be taking on a lot of extra duties as host—from finding a deserving charity to securing a location and soliciting local businesses for raffle prizes. Your job will seem never-ending. All the same, the rewards may well be worth it. To ensure a great night of fun and increase your odds of raising a chunk of charitable change that you can feel proud of, consider the following:

- Start planning two months ahead of time.

- Decide if the event will be private or open to the public.

- If you're holding the event at a bar or restaurant, ask the owner if he or she will match cash donations collected at the door, or if the establishment will provide a special menu and donate the proceeds. (TIP: Bar and restaurant owners typically get free or discounted liquor from distributors trying to build up new business. Ask if they can make a special drink or shot that will keep their costs down—and quickly build your donation.)

- Hold a raffle. Secure donated prizes from local businesses and sell raffle tickets to your guests. Call out winning ticket numbers throughout the night, and if you're able to secure a "grand prize," be sure to announce it several times. You can say something like,

"We'll pick another winning ticket in twenty minutes, and don't forget our grand prize drawing for the *insert awesome prize here* will be at *insert awesome specific time here.*" (TIP: To help secure prizes, provide prospective donors with the contact info for the charity you will be raising money for.)

☝ As much as your guests will want to get loaded up and have a good time, the host and perhaps a few friends should manage the event sober. Always keep an eye on the donated prizes and giveaways, and keep newly arriving guests informed of the prizes and special menu options.

SOME DO'S AND DON'TS FOR OFFICE PARTIES

Do: Take advantage of all acceptable workplace "goof-off time"

Don't: Be the person that shows up with a beer bong/eggnog bong

Do: Suggest the idea of a Secret Santa gift exchange

Don't: Assume it's acceptable to buy a gift from a lingerie/adult novelty store

Do: Offer to help set up decorations, bring food, or clean up after

Don't: Go near the copy machine. You know what we're talking about. It's just too tempting.

The Office Party

Another popular choice is the office party. There are some things we really like and other things we really hate about holding a party at your workplace. Openly wasting company time is a luxury rarely afforded, and seeing your boss wearing "Moose Battle" is kind of like waking up and finding Bigfoot making omelets in your kitchen. As much fun as it sounds, everyone has to consider the often-dangerous blend of work and alcohol. After too many eggnogs, you may find yourself finally being able to muster the courage to ask out Rhonda the receptionist, but you may also find yourself punching out Frank the snarky IT guy.

A Family Affair

Turning your annual family holiday gathering into an Ugly Christmas Sweater Party is the easiest of options. Since you are guaranteed to have pretty much the same guests show up year after year, whether you want them to or not, all you have to do is change the dress code. This can be a great way to see a lighter, more fun side of your family. Sure, Uncle Bob will still stand way too close as he tells you the same story about how he "could've really been somebody if it weren't for Aunt Vicky," but at least it will be more tolerable as he stands there wearing a neon green cardigan with "Ho! Ho! Ho!" written across the back in puffy paint and glitter. After you all get accustomed to some newfound Christmas fashion flair, as well as incorporate some games and activities (**SEE CHAPTER 2**), your family may grow closer than ever.

The Pub Crawl

The latest trend for Ugly Christmas Sweater Parties is the pub crawl. A roving party of sorts, the pub crawl consists of your gathering up your closest friends and family, hopping from bar to bar, and downing holiday-themed shots. As the night wears on, don't be surprised if complete

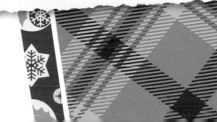

strangers get caught up in the hoopla and hop on the bandwagon o' fun. We suggest plotting out your path in an area that has a high concentration of bars within walking distance. There are a couple of reasons for this: First, drinking and driving will surely place your name high atop Santa's naughty list; and second, the credo of leaving no man behind is best left for those serving in the military, not those being served whiskey. Don't be discouraged when a partygoer wants to stay for another drink or try another pick-up line. They can meet you at the next stop on your route.

INVITES

Once you have chosen the type of party you will be throwing, you need to figure out when your party will take place and whom to invite. Obviously, the holiday season is a busy time and choosing a date that works for everyone is like trying to find an occasion where jean shorts are considered suitable attire: It's just not going to happen. However, it's best to capitalize on the Christmas spirit by hosting your party anywhere from the day after Thanksgiving until New Year's Day.

After selecting your party date, getting the word out about your Ugly Christmas Sweater Party is your next priority. Every host's biggest fear is throwing a party that nobody shows up to, but you can squash your fears by using this list.

See Facing Page

If you want your guests to show up in the most flamboyant and colorful of Ugly Christmas Sweaters, your invitations should be equally flamboyant and colorful. If your invitation is sent via snail mail, try adding glitter, sparkles, or anything else that can't be ignored at first glance. If you use Evite, you can add animation, music, and numerous other attention-grabbing devices to generate anticipation among your potential guests. This is your opportunity to set the tone for your event well in advance. Give your guests an idea of what qualifies as an Ugly Christmas Sweater, and where to get one, by including a link to www.UglyChristmasSweaterParty.com.

So your invites are out and the RSVPs are starting to come in. Now it's time to focus on what your guests will eat and what they will do at your Ugly Christmas Sweater Party.

Method	Pros	Cons
Evite	Quick; free; lets you easily track expected guests	Can get caught by spam filters; can appear cheap or impersonal
Smoke Signals	Can be seen for miles; enable you to get rid of leaves and communicate with friends at the same time	May burn down your house; not good for the ozone layer; may be against town ordinances
Snail Mail	Very personal; customizable; people can put the invite up on the fridge as a constant reminder	Slow; costly; may cause you to develop envelope tongue
Social Media	Friends list is readily available; easy to track; free	May be overlooked; may seem impersonal; may cause you to realize that while you have 585 friends online, you truly only have about 30
Carrier Pigeon	Your friends will receive an invitation from a carrier pigeon—enough said	You'll need time; energy; and money to train pigeons; invites might not go to intended person; someone might get bird flu
Phone Call	Personal; has minimal carbon footprint; long-distance rates have decreased	Limited minutes; risk of injuries relating to prolonged phone use; time-consuming if you use a rotary phone
Message in a Bottle	Alternative recycling method; great excuse to rid yourself of cork collection; relatively cheap	Slow; invitees must live near body of water; low delivery success rate
Town Crier	Reaches the masses; is attention-grabbing; unique	Expensive; hard to find good town criers these days; anyone within earshot may show up

ugly sing-along

Get the (Ugly) Party Started:
MUSIC, GAMES, AND ACTIVITIES

Who doesn't like music, games, and activities? If you answered "Me" to this question, then do us and everyone who knows you a favor: Put down this book and slap yourself in the face. Go ahead. We will wait.

OK. Feel better?

Music, games, and activities make everything more interesting. Why do you think millions of people flock to local carnivals every summer? It's not for the rickety rides manned by toothless weirdoes who reek of cheese and cigarettes. It's for the games and activities staffed by toothless weirdos who reek of cheese and cigarettes. Please keep this in mind as you plan your party. Sure, it can be successful without games and activities, but if you include even a few small, fun events, you will give your guests an experience rarely had at the usual humdrum holiday party, and they will beg you to make your shindig an annual event.

MUSIC

The selection of a sound track for your party is pretty self-explanatory, but for the sake of those who lack self-explanation skills, it's this: Plan on playing Christmas music, and only Christmas music. This is not the time to show off your collection of über-hip indie records. Stick to traditional holiday music. We are aware of the fact that by the time your party rolls around your guests have probably heard "Have a Holly, Jolly Christmas" a kajillion times, but we don't care. If people go to a Christmas party, they expect to hear Christmas music.

GAMES AND ACTIVITIES

When it comes to planning games and activities for your Ugly Christmas Sweater Party, keep things simple yet fun. If you have to gather everyone and force them to be quiet while you read off a long list of instructions, they will lose interest and you will be cutting into valuable party time. Remember, you are going to be explaining a game, not how to dismantle a nuclear bomb. Here are a few game ideas that are wildly entertaining and easy to explain and understand.

Holiday Name Tags

This game is played by placing a name tag on the back of each guest. On this name tag, write the name of a character from any Christmas movie, song, or book. The character can be really well-known or really obscure, but whatever you do, don't let the person whose tag it is see it. Each guest will have to figure out his or her name by asking the other guests Yes or No questions. Once guests guess the name correctly, they can move the name tag to the front of their sweater and pick a prize or get their party favor. Here is an example.

HELLO
my name is

Party Guest 1: Am I an animal?

Party Guest 2: No.

Party Guest 1: Am I a person?

Party Guest 2: Yes.

Party Guest 1: I'm Rudolph, aren't I?

Party Guest 2: You suck at this game.

This type of conversation is sure to take place at your party, but folks will figure things out eventually. As an added bonus, it is fun to watch someone grow angrier and angrier while trying in vain to guess a really hard name. This game is great for any party, but we recommend using this as an icebreaker at a charity event where the guests might not all know one another.

Christmas Movie Trivia

Type up a list of questions based on popular Christmas movies, such as *A Christmas Story*, *It's a Wonderful Life*, and *National Lampoon's Christmas Vacation*. Quiz your guests throughout the night, or have them pair off into teams for a period of time. The first to answer correctly wins a prize or earns a point. If you go with the point system, the guest who has the most points at the end of the night wins the prize. You can make your questions as easy or as difficult as you like. We like to start with a few easy ones, then gradually increase the difficulty. This keeps people engaged and knocks the Noel Know-It-Alls down a few pegs. Here are some examples of what your questions should look like.

We love the Christmas movie trivia idea because it's an easy game to implement and can either be used as a main attraction or sprinkled in throughout the night to complement your other games. Everyone loves Christmas movies, and your guests will all think they know the answers, so you will need to have keen eyes and sharp ears to know who gets the answers first.

1.
In the Christmas classic *It's a Wonderful Life*, what happens whenever a bell rings?

2.
In *A Christmas Story*, what was Ralphie's brother's name?

3.
What is the name of Cousin Eddie's dog in *National Lampoon's Christmas Vacation*?

4.
In Charles Dickens's *A Christmas Carol*, what is the name of Scrooge's deceased business partner?

5.
In the 1964 classic *Rudolph the Red-Nosed Reindeer*, what was the name of the elf who wanted to be a dentist?

GIFT EXCHANGE

The giving and receiving of gifts can be one of the best aspects of the holiday season. Imagine how much fun it would be if the ritual were the giving, receiving, and *taking away* of gifts?

We have two types of gift exchanges that may leave you and your guests with some great gifts, or may leave you with resentment toward your brother-in-law for taking away the copy of *Rush Hour 3* you have been waiting all year for. Either way, these gift exchanges are sure to have partygoers talking for some time.

Dirty Dice Gift Exchange

This exchange requires each participant to gather around a table while in possession of a pair of dice. You also need a timer and an assortment of small gifts such as DVDs, books, or CDs—anything that can be placed in the middle of a table and passed around quickly. The wrapped gifts should be desirable, so that people will want them, and there doesn't necessarily have to be a price limit—watches, iPods, ties, and purses are all great ideas as well.

Have participants gather around the table, set the timer for two minutes, and then have participants try to roll two of any kind. Once a player rolls two of a kind, he or she may then, and only then, take a present from the center of the table and place it in front of him- or herself. The player may then resume rolling the dice and grabbing more gifts until the two minutes are up. If all of the gifts have been taken from the middle of the table, players may then grab gifts from other players once they have rolled two of a kind. Once the time is up, players may open and keep any gift that is left in front of them.

Bad Santa Gift Exchange

Tell everyone you invite to buy and bring a wrapped gift of a specified nominal value. Usually gifts between $20 and $30 are appropriate, depending on if you are having a family or work party. All of the gifts are placed in the center of the room in a pile. Each participant draws a number from a hat to determine the order in which they will select gifts. The player with the lowest number unfortunately gets to start things off. He or she picks a present from the pile and unwraps it. Once this first gift has been opened, the next player has the option of opening a new present from the center pile or instead taking away the first player's gift—and things go on from there. If someone's chosen gift is taken by another participant, he or she must go back to the central pile and open up a new present. This continues until all of the gifts are opened and in the possession of one of your happy—or at this point, not-so-happy—partygoers.

Simple party favors that jolly or jilted guests take home with them can remind them of the fun they had or alleviate the pain of having a gift ripped from their hands. Partygoers will be snapping plenty of pictures, so help them capture the ugliness by providing a tacky picture frame. Give each guest a gaudy ornament to hang on their tree, or see if you can find personalized mini snow globes with sweater-clad carolers.

DECORATIONS

Finally, ambiance is something else to consider. It's an activity for the eyes. Be sure to hang plenty of mistletoe and decorate accordingly. You don't have to go full-on Clark Griswold, but small knickknacks scattered around really add a nice touch. The tackier the decorations are, the better. Move the crappy ornaments that your kids made in kindergarten from the back of your tree to the front for all to enjoy, or bring the outside in by filling empty corners with the cheap plastic Santas and reindeer that are usually relegated to roofs and front yards. If there's a television in the room, we recommend popping in a DVD of a Yule log burning with accompanying holiday music.

By providing remarkable décor along with games and activities for your guests to take part in, you will not only be providing hours of entertainment, you will also be laying the foundation for what may very well become one of the most talked-about parties of the year.

Ugly
FOOD AND DRINKS

We all know that the quickest way to partygoers' hearts is through their stomachs, unless you happen to be a heart surgeon—then you are well aware that the quickest way is with a bone saw, surgical clamps, and a scalpel. Offering your guests an abundance of epicurean delights is the best way to ensure your party will be a success. Depending on which type of host you are, you will find that menu planning can be as easy as ordering a dozen pizzas or as difficult as cooking a seven-course gourmet meal. Unless, of course, you are in college, in which case you can just put out a jar of pickles and skip to the Ugly Drinks portion of this chapter (**SEE PAGE 26**).

By the time the guests start to arrive at your party, you have most likely put in hours of hard work preparing for it. The last thing you want to do is stand at the head of the buffet line carving pieces of prime rib. You want to be able to mingle with your guests and enjoy the fruits of your labor. A self-service spread of food and drink can help assure that you will be in the mix of Ugly-Christmas-Sweater—wearing patrons instead of behind a bar mixing drinks for everyone else.

While we have no desire to write a cookbook, unless it is a cookbook about the forty seven different meals you can make with nacho chips, pepperoni slices, and shredded cheese at 3:30 A.M., we have gathered some of our favorite Ugly Christmas Sweater Party food and drink recipes to share with you. Since not very many of you are executive chefs, we have designed these not only to tantalize your fellow Uglies' taste buds, but also to be easy to whip together. For those of you who *are* executive chefs, if you are seriously reading our chapter on food and drinks, you may want to consider another profession.

UGLY FOOD

One of our favorite Ugly Christmas Sweater Party snacks is something we call Coniferous Confections. Not only are they sure to win over your guests, but they double as decorations. Coniferous Confections are our take on the traditional Rice Krispies Treats, but with a holiday spin in the form of a Christmas tree. Finally—a party where it is not frowned upon to eat the decorations!

CONIFEROUS CONFECTIONS

makes six cones

3 tablespoons butter or margarine
32 large marshmallows or 3 cups miniature marshmallows
1/2 teaspoon vanilla
1/2 teaspoon green food coloring
4 cups dry toasted oats cereal
About 12 small gumdrops (enough to cover all 6 cones)
Small bowl of very hot water

DIRECTIONS

Heat butter and marshmallows in a saucepan over medium heat until melted. Remove from heat and stir in vanilla and food coloring. Fold in cereal and mix until it is evenly coated. Using buttered hands, quickly shape warm mixture into triangular tree shapes and place them on a piece of waxed paper. For ornaments, thinly slice gumdrops and press them onto the trees. Let sit or eat right away.

Hint: To ease the stickiness of the gumdrops, keep the small bowl of very hot water nearby and continually dip your knife in it as you slice the gumdrops.

Everyone loves bacon. Those of you who say you don't like bacon, do in fact like bacon. Your taste buds are just liars. With that being said, here is our favorite holiday bacon appetizer, Reindeer Nuts. For those of you trying to watch your girlish figure, try using turkey bacon. But don't blame us if one of your guests leaves you with an upper decker for not serving real bacon.

REINDEER NUTS

16 ounces bacon strips, cut into thirds
Two 8-ounce cans water chestnuts
Barbecue sauce
Wooden toothpicks

DIRECTIONS

Preheat oven to 400°F. Wrap each piece of bacon around one water chestnut, secure with wooden toothpick, and place on baking sheet. Repeat until sheet is full. Bake until bacon looks just about done, then mop on your favorite barbecue sauce and continue to cook until crisp.

CHRISTMAS CHEESE BALLS

Two 8-ounce blocks cream cheese, softened
8 generous dashes garlic powder
4 tablespoons mayonnaise
Dash lemon juice
8 green onions
12 slices pastrami or corned beef

DIRECTIONS
Place softened cream cheese in a mixing bowl. Add garlic powder, mayonnaise, and lemon juice; set aside. Finely dice green onions and pastrami. Add to cream cheese mixture and blend with clean hands. Form into an oblong log, chill, and serve with your favorite crackers.

Hint: This log may be rolled in finely chopped walnuts or pecans ("bark"); however, we prefer to leave the log exposed to show the festive red and green Christmas colors.

One thing is for sure: You'd better make sure that the sweaters are not the only cheesy things floating around your party. Cheese is a staple of any good spread of food. Whether it is served in chunks, curds, slices, or finely grated over the gelatin mold, cheese is a must. If you do, in fact, find yourself standing over the gelatin mold with a cheese grater, reach for the following ball of fun.

Whether you choose to use some of our gourmet recipes or bake your not-so-famous Brussels sprout soufflé, make sure to have enough food for your guests to gorge themselves on. We all know what happens when Uncle Rico drinks on an empty stomach, and nobody wants to be in county lockup wearing an Ugly Christmas Sweater. Not even Uncle Rico.

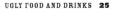

UGLY DRINKS

When it comes to the drinks, you cannot just plop a keg in the corner with some red plastic cups and consider the matter taken care of. Unless, of course, your party is being held in a double-wide, in which case please check out our children's book, *Santa Doesn't Visit Trailer Parks Because There Aren't Any Chimneys*.

We aren't saying you can't have a keg of your favorite pilsner. We are saying you should include some of your favorite holiday-themed cocktails as well. Nobody expects to show up at your shindig and see you flinging bottles through the air like Tom Cruise in *Cocktail*, but mixing up some tasty concoctions is easier than you may think. Given that an Ugly Christmas Sweater Party is a holiday party, we suggest you mix up some holiday spirits. The first thing that comes to mind when everyone thinks about holiday drinks is, of course, the Shamrock Shake from McDonald's. The second is eggnog.

Eggnog

Eggnog is a surefire way to get everybody in the holiday spirit, and, depending on how strong you make it, out of their Ugly Christmas Sweaters. We were faced with the daunting task of sampling numerous eggnog recipes to find out which one we should share with you. After we sobered up, apologized to the neighbors, and returned the goat to the farmer down the street, we picked our favorite.

EGGNOG RECIPE

12 eggs
1 quart milk
1 pint heavy cream
1 teaspoon vanilla extract
1 pint whiskey
1 cup white sugar
Ground nutmeg to taste

DIRECTIONS

Separate egg yolks and egg whites into two bowls. Set aside bowl with egg whites. In a large bowl, mix milk, cream, egg yolks, vanilla, and whiskey by hand until smooth and creamy. Gradually add sugar while continuing to whip until mixture is stiff. Fold egg whites into egg yolk mixture, and pour into a punch bowl. Serve in mugs garnished with a dash of nutmeg.

Energizer Elf

A belly full of food and eggnog can leave people feeling warm and fuzzy inside, but it may also leave some feeling quite drowsy. Before you reach for that coffee pot and ruin a perfectly good buzz, why not offer your guests a pick-me-up that won't leave them sober and wondering how much longer they have to stay? Instead, whip them up an alcoholic energy drink. We do suggest that you are selective while handing these out, though. If you think your mother-in-law is an annoying drunk, just wait until you see her drunk and alert.

Here is an easy way to keep your party hoppin' into the wee hours of the night.

ENERGIZER ELF RECIPE

5 ounces any green-colored energy drink (per serving)
1 ounce vodka (per serving)
1 peppermint stick (per serving)

DIRECTIONS

Pour energy drink and vodka into shaker filled with ice to chill. Shake for 30 seconds, then pour into glass filled with ice. Garnish with peppermint stick.

Everyone Gets Blitzened

No party is complete without a giant punch bowl filled with some sort of fruity, tasty, mystery mixture. Now it is up to you to determine how much of this bowl is filled with fruit drinks, and how much of it is filled with the good stuff. Keep in mind, however, that the amount of alcohol in the bowl has been scientifically proven to be heavily correlated with the success of your party. That being said, we leave you with one of our secret weapons from our Ugly Christmas Sweater Party arsenal of drinks: Everyone Gets Blitzened. It's not just a funny play on words, either; it's a foregone conclusion. Take the keys away from everyone you see drinking from this bowl of broth. You may also want to pin peoples' home addresses onto their Ugly Christmas Sweaters, because they may not be speaking too clearly, or at all, by the time they get in a cab.

EVERYONE GETS BLITZENED RECIPE

Three .75-liter bottles vodka
Two .75-liter bottles Bacardi 151 rum
One .75-liter bottle peppermint schnapps
One .75-liter bottle sour apple schnapps
One .75-liter bottle triple sec
One .75-liter bottle gin
Four .75-liter bottles Boone's Farm Strawberry Hill Wine
8 liters fruit punch
Five 2-liter bottles lemon-lime soda
1 liter orange juice
Two 12-ounce cans orange juice concentrate

DIRECTIONS

Mix all ingredients in large punch bowl. Chill with ice. Stand back
and watch party start.

CHAPTER 4

Bring on the Ugly:
WHAT TO WEAR

?

In today's day and age, when appearance is everything, attending an Ugly Christmas Sweater Party is your chance to rebel against the strong arm of the fashion law. Dressing ugly on purpose goes against everything we have ever been taught about the do's and don'ts of style, and we are confident that you will find it freeing and fun. This is your chance to finally mix plaids with stripes, and blacks with browns, or wear socks with sandals. What we are saying is that when it comes to dressing ugly, anything goes and the possibilities are endless.

CHOOSING AN UGLY CHRISTMAS SWEATER

Everything these days seems to come with a rule book or a set of instructions, except for ice cube trays. (If anyone has figured out how to get the cubes out once frozen, please e-mail us at uglychristmassweaterpartysales@gmail.com.) While there are no guidelines for dressing ugly, there certainly are for choosing the right Ugly Christmas Sweater. We have a few tips that will ensure you will be in the running for worst dressed.

When choosing an Ugly Christmas Sweater, your main goal should be to stimulate as many of the five senses as possible. You will want to pick a sweater that is so retina-burning colorful that the only way people will be able to look at you is through one of those foil-covered boxes that middle school students make so they can look at a solar eclipse. But color alone isn't going to win any contests. You'll want to break into the third dimension. The more stuff you have hanging off your sweater, the better. For instance, lights, trees, stockings, candy canes, and even Santa's beard, if you are stealthy enough to sneak up on him and cut it off, can be flowing from your sweater. Your goal is to walk in looking like a sniper trying to blend in with a Christmas tree.

While the sight of an Ugly Christmas Sweater is sure to grab everyone's attention, the sound of an Ugly Christmas Sweater must not be overlooked. Whether your sound track is a talking Santa, a set of chimes, or a Salvation Army bell-ringer you have somehow managed to sew on to your sweater, you want partygoers to hear you coming. An easy and effective method of getting this done is fastening jingle bells or any other Christmas-related noisemaker to your attire. If it rings, whistles, rattles, or sings, find a way to attach it to your sweater!

Once you have the audio and visual components of your sweater taken care of, it's time to get really creative. Finding a way to make your sweater interactive will set you apart from other guests. The objective here is authenticity. If you have a cone-bearing tree depicted on your sweater, try attaching real pinecones. If Santa's reindeer adorn your sweater, try adding real reindeer fur. (If you plan on doing this, we highly suggest checking out our other book, *The Art of Reindeer Shearing*.) The idea is to have people not only wanting to look at your sweater but also touch it, and placing real objects on your sweater will surely get people playing with or petting your sweater all night.

But beware of where you place the objects. You don't want Mr. or Mrs. Grabby Hands touching you in places you don't want to be touched.

Holiday Sausages

This game is played by dividing your guests into two teams. A player from Team 1 may ask any question of any player on Team 2. The player from Team 2 has to answer the question with the phrase "Holiday Sausages," no matter what the question is. If the player is able to say "Holiday Sausages" without laughing, Team 2 gets a point. Think it sounds too easy? Let's give it a shot.

TEAM UGLY:

Hey, Reader, thanks for buying our book. What is that thing crammed into your pants?

YOU:

(Trying to hold back laughter...)
(Still trying...)

...H-H-Holi-...

(erupting in laughter)

POINT FOR US!

This is a great game to play with family and friends at any house party as long as you can stomach hearing your grandmother repeat the word "sausages" over and over.

CHOOSING A WINNING UGLY CHRISTMAS SWEATER

If your plan is to go to a party and have a good time, you can pretty much quit reading at this point. You've accomplished your Ugly Christmas Sweater mission. However, if your plan is to go home with the first-place prize, it is time to touch on the last two senses: taste and smell.

Warning:

!

This is for the uninhibited, because you will have people coming at you with their mouths.

Turn yourself into a moving snack platter by affixing gumdrops, candy canes, gingerbread men, or any other holiday goodie that you so desire. Try to stay away from anything that may melt or rot, such as chocolates or leftover Christmas ham. No one wants to be the smelly rotting meat guy at the party. What you do want to smell like is a mixture of fresh-baked cookies,

Christmas trees, and fruitcake. Before you leave for the party, set aside the fancy perfumes and try dabbing a little vanilla extract behind your ears, or give yourself a thorough rubdown with the pine-scented air freshener in your car.

Accessorize, Accessorize, Accessorize!

At some parties, simply showing up in an Ugly Christmas Sweater won't win you any prizes. This is where creative accessorizing can set you apart. Use your whole body as a canvas for head-to-toe ugliness. A bright pair of plaid or holiday-print pants can really accent the ugliness of your sweater. To hold up your ugly pants, refashion a strand of workable Christmas lights into a practical belt (make sure that your repurposed belt still does the same thing as a standard belt, though; crack still kills at Ugly Christmas Sweater Parties).

Light-up necklaces, earrings, and bracelets are also par for the course. A standard Santa hat will work, but try looking for elf ears or reindeer antlers to wear on your brain container. Consider turtlenecks, too—an often-underutilized ugly tool. Turtlenecks work great under almost all sweaters, especially vests and cardigans, where you can really show off the tacky holiday print. Don't worry about matching, either; clashing colors and prints only add to the ugly!

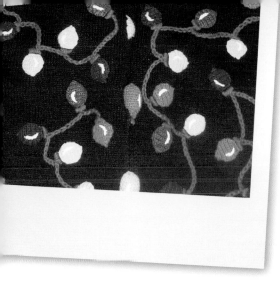

THINK UGLY, NOT STUPID

If you have managed to hit on all five senses, you are assured to have one of the best sweaters (if not *the* best) at the party. While constructing this monstrosity, keep in mind you will have to wear it for an extended period of time. Comfort and safety are vital to fully enjoying the party. Wearing five hundred jingle bells on your person will be sure to have everyone talking, but it may also have you reaching for some headache medicine. You should make sure all pins are securely fastened in a safe manner, because people bleed faster as they drink more. If you are partying in a warm-weather climate, avoid layering, and think twice about wearing that wool turtleneck. This would instead be the perfect opportunity to wear an ugly vest sans undershirt. Wherever you go in your Noisy, Eye-Popping, Touchy-Feely Ugly Christmas Sweater, another important thing to remember is to stay away from open flames. At this point you have become highly flammable, and you can easily be turned into a human Yule log. The bottom line is that if you are not comfortable in your getup, it can ruin a good night fast. Make sure you have a full range of motion so you don't end up like Rudolph, left out of all the reindeer games.

If you are having problems determining what qualifies as an Ugly Christmas Sweater, we recommend visiting our website, where you can view thousands of the world's ugliest sweaters and pictures of partygoers in their ugliest attire. Or just flip to chapter 7.

CHAPTER 5

What to Expect When You're Expecting Ugly:

WHO WILL BE THERE

WITH AN INTRODUCTION TO THE SWEATER IDENTITY PARADOX THEORY

As host, you normally know in advance who will be attending your party. After all, you have sent out invites and received RSVPs. However, with Ugly Christmas Sweater Parties, there is still some mystery involved. Yes, you will know who everyone is at your party, but in our experience, people take on different personas when it comes to the Ugly Christmas Sweater Party. To be fully prepared, you need to know what classification they fall into. You need our Sweater Identity Paradox Theory.

The SIPT was born when we discovered friends and family, whom we thought we actually knew, behaving in ways that didn't necessarily match their personalities. Our fun friends were dressed in understated sweaters and not fully buying into the party, while our more reserved friends showed up in full-on, head-to-toe ugliness and dove headfirst into the world of Ugly Christmas Sweater Parties.

After extensive research, we sent NASA our bar graphs and pie charts* in order to prove that Ugly Christmas Sweaters were some sort of portal to a tangential universe, or at the very least a wormhole in the space-time continuum. The data is still being analyzed.

For now, we will not go into the science of the SIPT, but will simply lay out for you the different classifications you can expect to find at your party.

ALL-OUT ALLEN

Decked out from head to toe, All-Out Allen can be expected to show up wearing not only an Ugly Christmas Sweater, but ugly pants, hat, reindeer ears, shoes with bells, and anything else associated with Christmas.

Natural Environment: You're most likely to run into an All-Out Allen at a party held on a college campus or on a pub crawl.

Warnings: When you encounter an All-Out Allen, be prepared for heavy usage of the words *bro*, *dude*, and *gnarly*.

---

* In retrospect, we feel we could have gotten a quicker response from NASA if our graphs and charts weren't written on napkins.

CRAFTY SAM

Duct tape, check. Hot glue gun, check. This do-it-yourselfer can whip up a festive getup for any party.

Natural Environment: Besides Hobby Lobby, a Crafty Sam is most likely to be found at a house or office party.

Warnings: When around a Crafty Sam, use extreme caution. He or she will be highly flammable, and you may get a contact high from the glue emanating from the sweater.

LAST-MINUTE LANCE

Everyone knows this guy. He is the one who puts off everything until the last minute, so he's forced to scramble around town looking for anything that can pass as an Ugly Christmas Sweater. He

may show up in a plain red sweater, or he could get lucky and find a gem. You never know with a Last-Minute Lance.

Natural Environment: Most likely a bar party or pub crawl. A Last-Minute Lance will never be able to RSVP on time.

Warnings: May ask you to borrow money or buy him a beer.

COPYCAT COLLIN

Oh, you're wearing a turtleneck with a vest? Sweet. . . . Me too.

Natural Environment: A Copycat Collin can be found at any variety of Ugly Christmas Sweater Party.

Warnings: If you are wearing the same outfit as Copycat Collin, prepare yourself for endless photos and nonstop jokes from fellow partygoers.

TOO COOL TRACY

Too Cool Tracy takes herself way too seriously to ever wear an Ugly Christmas Sweater. She will, however, go to a party just to make snide remarks about others. She sucks.

Natural Environment: Too Cool Tracy can be found at any Ugly Christmas Sweater Party held by graduate students or hipsters.

Warnings: Will want to discuss the socioeconomic ramifications of throwing an Ugly Christmas Sweater Party, might have hairy armpits, and might smell of patchouli oil.

INADVERTENT ELLEN

This woman hasn't a clue. She shows up to the office party sporting a potential award-winner, yet can't stop repeating, "I don't get what's so ugly about this."

Natural Environment: Any office, elementary school, library, or Kohl's department store. Inadvertent Ellen will never be found at an Ugly Christmas Sweater Party on purpose.

Warnings: Any conversation entered into with an Inadvertent Ellen will involve her cats and/or grandchildren; however, she will have an excellent selection of hard candies at the ready.

EARLY BIRD BLAKE

Expect to see this guy camping out and running all over for Black Friday deals in his Ugly Christmas Sweater Party gear. And, like those extra five pounds, he keeps his gear on throughout the holidays.

Natural Environment: At any and every party he can attend. An Early Bird Blake will somehow manage to hit every party in town and have a different outfit for each one.

Warnings: Don't let an Early Bird Blake drive anywhere, for he is more than likely chemically dependent on cocaine.

THAT COUPLE

"Do you want to go?" "I don't know. . . . Do you want to go?" "Maybe we should go. . . . I don't have anything ugly to wear."
"I hate parties. . . . I'm going to look stupid. Are you sure we should go?" "Let's just go to JC Penney and buy something."

Natural Environment: That Couple will only be seen at a house party before 8 P.M. After that, parenting duties call. The woman will tell the guy that he can stay and hang with his friends, but he knows she doesn't really mean it and he'll hear about it tomorrow if he does stay.

Warnings: You will be forced to look at baby pictures and hear about how advanced their child is and how it's the first time they have ever left the baby alone with a sitter.

DRANK TOO MUCH BRANDY BRANDY

Look out! She's the biggest fan of eggnog—until it ends up as a huge stain on your rug.

Natural Environment: Anywhere that serves booze.

Warnings: In a perpetual state of intoxication, Drank Too Much Brandy Brandy will pepper you with questions about why you never call her, and will more than likely cry at one point in the evening

The Contest:

JUDGING THE BEST
OF THE UGLIEST

"Winning isn't everything—it's the only thing."

It has been said that Coach Vince Lombardi spoke these words to motivate his Green Bay Packers, but the truth is that he actually inked these famous words on the bottom of his Ugly Christmas Sweater Party invitations to inspire his guests to go for the top prize. History may never reveal whether or not Lombardi won any championships, but one thing is for sure: That guy could throw one hell of an Ugly Christmas Sweater Party!

IT'S MY PARTY AND I'LL JUDGE IF I WANT TO

After all of the preparation and decoration, the party will not be complete without nomination and congratulation. We're referring to the climax of the evening: awarding a prize to the guest who's wearing the ugliest sweater.

There are many approaches to officially crowning a victor, and while all will work, the following options will prove to have varying degrees of effectiveness depending on the type of Ugly Christmas Sweater Party being thrown.

⚖ **Applause:** This method is very efficient for larger crowds. Those who wish to compete can either nominate themselves or be shoved onstage by a friend. The host moves throughout the competitors and waits for the audience to react. Scientifically sound? Not exactly. Democratic? Kind of. Is it a quick and easy way to find the ugliest in attendance? Without question.

⚖ **Panel of Judges:** Everyone can compete and campaign, but ultimately, true ugly will be determined by an appointed crew of experts.* Consider the fun when, at your family's next Ugly Christmas Sweater Party, the contest has a panel of judges made up of the following trio: your ninety-four-year-old crazy grandmother; your cousin's girlfriend, who also happens to be your other cousin's ex-girlfriend; and your twelve-year-old nephew, who is very open to taking bribes.

*We recommend using caution when saying to someone, "Hey, you seem to know a lot about ugly things."

🖐 **Celebrity Judge:** This is an exciting twist to the Panel of Judges method, with a variety of applications. Perhaps you're planning a large Ugly Christmas Sweater Party fundraiser and hope to increase the attendance (and funds raised); consider inviting a politician, sports figure, or hometown hero who's made it to the big time to attend your event and participate as a celebrity judge. Be sure to provide as many details as possible regarding who will benefit from the fundraiser, and offer plenty of advance notice.

🖐 **Secret Ballot:** Recommended for smaller groups, the secret ballot requires everyone in the room to know everyone else's name (or nickname), as the write-in vote for "Dude with the Ugly Christmas Sweater" or "Creepy Guy with the Mustache" will get you all nowhere fast. If you would prefer to use the secret ballot method for a large group, we suggest providing numbered entry tags (like the ones you see marathon runners wear) or "Hello My Name Is" tags at the gate. Guests will have a blast coming up with creative names for their Ugly Christmas Sweaters, the activity acts as a great icebreaker, and once again you avoid getting back ballots that read "Short Chick with the Mustache." Once the guests cast their votes, the host can collect the ballots and tally up the results.

Deciding on the voting methodology is easy; the hard part is trying to figure out how you'll sort through all the ugly to find a true winner. But don't worry; we have developed some foolproof criteria.

- **Colors:** Green, red, and shades of white are a given, so look for shimmer and shine along with patterns that make your eyes water. If you're still not able to differentiate, turn to texture and custom homemade accessories for additional points.

- **Creatures from the North Pole:** Ugly Christmas Sweaters sporting a snowman or elf will cover the ante, but to win the pot a contestant has to have an ace up his or her sleeve. Look for the superior candidate to have a sweater with rare findings like Mrs. Claus, gingerbread men, or angry-looking reindeer that appear to have been exposed to high levels of radiation.

- **Lights and Sounds:** Will Ugly Christmas Sweater Parties ever stop? Yo, I don't know. Turn off the lights and my sweater will glow. Flashy and loud is what it's all about, so why not score a few extra-credit points to those who shine and provide their own holiday music?

THE CROWNING MOMENT:
THERE CAN BE ONLY ONE WINNER...
OR TWO...OR THREE

⚬ **Win, Place, and Showoff:** Just as every beauty pageant has a winner and first runner-up, so too shall your Ugly Christmas Sweater Party contest. There may be special duties required of the winner, and should he or she be unable to commit (or unwilling to pose for a controversial magazine) a replacement will be needed. Also, we like the idea of recognizing a "Showoff" who helped make the event memorable. Your choice may range from the attendee who made the largest charity contribution to the individual(s) who downed the most eggnog along the pub crawl route.

⚬ **Authentic Ugliness:** We often see Ugly Christmas Sweaters that were intentionally made with the most severe overusage of glitter, sparkles, and Santa Claus iron-on appliqués, but every so often an authentic piece of true ugly appears, and when it does, we suggest bowing to its greatness (that is, give the owner some type of blue ribbon). Typically these gems are knitted from the finest yarn a clearance aisle can produce, and

it's not uncommon to see sweaters featuring a random sampling of holiday images, such as reindeer or stockings hanging from a fireplace mantle, directly adjacent to not-so-holiday images such as kittens. Knitters love kittens. The stranger the combination of colors, materials, and images, the higher the ugly ranking should go.

⚬ **Most Crafty:** When Thomas Edison painted the Mona Lisa, he started out with a blank canvas. Well, some people are just gifted. In the world of Ugly Christmas Sweaters, there is a special breed of do-it-yourselfers that deserves to be recognized for their imaginative, and sometimes disturbing, minds. Contestants should be awarded for their creative incorporation of candy canes, mistletoe, ribbons, bells—and anything else that engages the five senses—into the Ugly Christmas Sweater Party experience.

♻ **Mechanically Gifted:** Often the most competitive and sought-after category to compete in is the one that brings out everyone's inner audio-visual geek. The "Clark Griswold Award" belongs to a special individual who likely spent way too much time and way too much money to create a custom Ugly Christmas Sweater (or perhaps an entire outfit). This person's getup tends to be highly flammable, and depending on his or her knowledge of circuitry, could pose multiple hazards to self and others. No risk, no reward. The victor of this category should be fairly obvious to pick out.

wicked ugly

CHAPTER 7

The Ugly Christmas Sweater

HALL OF FAME

A Santa imposter has been reportedly slipping Rohypnol, aka roofies, into unsuspecting individuals' milk. Roofie Claus, as he is now known, steals all of the presents from under the tree once his victims have passed out. Roofie Claus is pictured here waiting for one of his many victims to fall into a deep slumber.

I BELIEVE IN Santa Claus

Roofie Claus

The Big Fat Fire Starter

Little is known about them, but Santa went through some dark years in the early 1900s. This sweater portrays a picture that was snapped of Santa by a Russian satellite in 1905. He served eleven months in a Russian prison for setting fire to these houses in a small village.

Killer Boots Man

It seems that the snowman in the red sweater has taken the other two hostage at branchpoint. Apparently, there was a discrepancy over why the larger snowman got to have legs and the other two didn't. The individual in the red decided that the boots would match his sweater nicely, and has been holding them at branchpoint ever since.

A River Runs Through It

While Christmas is usually a joyous time to spend with family and friends, this small town will be spending the holiday season filling sandbags. The mayor will surely be looking for a new job come reelection time after hiring that group of beavers to build the town dam.

With the way technology has been evolving throughout the years, it was only a matter of time before Santa found a new means of transportation. Prancer and his four-legged friends were sent off with a nice severance package. They are now working at an outsourced call center in India.

Prancer Gets Pink-slipped

Lift Me UP, Before You Go Go

Nothing says "Merry Christmas" like flying down a hill at an uncontrollable speed while trying to dodge evergreens and check out ski bunnies all at the same time. If you happen to make it to the bottom of the mountain in one piece, this sweater is waiting for you in the gift shop. What is worse, showing up the next day to work wearing this sweater, or sporting a cast on your freshly broken leg?

The Evolution of Penguin Dance

Penguins have spent the better part of the past century trying to perfect the art of dance. While their short flippers prove to be a slight disadvantage, their low centers of gravity more than make up for it. It has been rumored that Julia Stiles spent eight months in the Antarctic studying penguins' moves for her role in *Save the Last Dance*.

The confused look on this bear's face was not caused by the fact that it was raining candy canes; that is normal where he comes from. It's because his cheap grandma told him to carefully open his gifts without damaging the paper because she saves it and reuses it. *You* try opening a gift without ripping the paper when you have a set of claws and no opposable thumbs!

Beary Thrifty

RIGHT

This sweater has actually been outlawed in seven different states for the following reasons.

1. **It has been proven to trigger epileptic seizures.**

2. **It is believed that the gingerbread men come to life at night and are, in fact, ninjas.**

3. **It makes babies cry.**

FAR RIGHT

These snow parents hurry their children along while opening gifts on Christmas morning. Not because they are late to Grandma's for brunch, but because their children are clearly melting. Which brings me to why we are here today: For just $1 a day, you can help keep these kids from turning into nothing more than a dirty puddle.

In Living Color

I'm melting . . .

Layaway Santa

Cat Burglars

Everyone has heard of Santa's naughty or nice list. What most people have not heard of is the almost-but-not-quite-nice list. In this case, Santa leaves the children's gifts on top of the chimney instead of bringing them down. After spending Christmas morning hauling presents off the roof, the children learn the perks of being on the nice list.

At first glance, it may seem as though these cute little kittens are being mischievous and have found their way into the Christmas decorations. The sad truth is they work for an underground crime syndicate that deals in stolen holiday goods on the black market.

8-Bit Sweater

It's a good thing sweater manufacturing has evolved much like video game systems have. Some of the very first gaming systems were only 8 bit, which meant the images came across as looking very blocky and lacked any real detail, much like this sweater.

The big man recently had a surprise visit from the Occupational Safety and Health Administration after this sweater was released. He was cited for multiple infractions, including use of an extremely unsafe ladder, employees using presents as step stools, and not allowing his employees their 15-minute milk and cookie breaks.

The Safety Infraction Sweater Vest

RIGHT

Chastity belts were deemed unfashionable many years ago, not to mention they made women's bathroom lines unbearably long. Therefore, chastity sweaters were invented. These intimidating nutcrackers will be sure to ward off even the smoothest talking of playboys. After all, you can't get home without first rounding second base.

FAR RIGHT

We are all aware that the economy has been rough at best over the past few years, but really, Santa? Don't just stand there with your arms in the air and that look of defeat on your face. The kids still need their presents. It's not their fault you lost your ass in the real estate collapse.

You Shall Not Pass

Old Saint Vagabond

After hundreds of years being rolled up, dressed up, and left in the front yard only to slowly wither away, Frosty has officially lost it. He is suffering from an extreme personality disorder, sometimes even dressing in drag. Next time you see him, just let him know you care.

Schizophrenic Snowmen

The 101st Battalion of Para-Penguins are pictured here descending at the 75th Annual South Pole Air & Water Show. This year they entertained the record crowd of fourteen while taking a break from the same war they have been fighting for years: global warming.

Para-Penguins

Fire Exit

It is always a good idea to have a giant bright-red door for your family to be able to locate easily in case of a fire. Especially when a house fire is imminent because you think it's a good idea to hang a giant flammable stocking over your roaring fireplace.

Nothing says "Merry Christmas" like pastel colors, right? Wrong. This sweater's manufacturer obviously had fabric left over from his Easter Sweaters and thought he could pull a fast one on unsuspecting consumers. The only thing they pulled was their company's sign off of the front of their building when they went out of business.

merry Eastermas

Buffets are perfect for those individuals who go to restaurants and end up staring at the menu for a half an hour because they can't choose what they want. Whoever made this sweater is definitely one of those individuals.

You don't have to be a rocket scientist to figure out that those flimsy wings would not be able to lift those hefty snowmen off of the ground. So if it isn't those wings that got them so high, what was it?

Christmas Buffet

Angel Dust

Snowmen Wobble but They Don't Fall Down

Not So Bad News Bears

LEFT

It is said that the majority of Americans are overweight and unhealthy. After conducting a very unscientific survey, we have found that the majority of Americans have a fear of being pushed over. Evolution has tried to combat this fear by creating rounder humans. Like these snowmen, if pushed, they wobble but they don't fall down.

ABOVE

At first glance you may think that these three are a force to be reckoned with. It turns out, however, that they are all roar and no bite. They have just been taking pictures of themselves standing next to really small trees so they look big and tough in their Facebook pictures.

From my Head to Bows

Suppose your clothes were covered with bows. Your love for tying ribbon certainly shows.

Is that train really balancing on one rail? The teddy bear looks possessed, and as if things weren't creepy enough, check out what's going on in the background. Which is scarier, the plaid couch or the dolly the size of a tween?

Not to Scale

Not Too Sure What my True
Love Gave to me

Illustrating the "Twelve Days of Christmas" should be easy, but there are so many things wrong here: a 9 next to the drums, when the lyrics clearly state "12 drummers drumming," and what's up with the 10 next to a violin? Better yet, what's up with the violin?

Snowmen cosmetic surgeons agree that carrots are so last year and that construction cones are the new rage.

Nice to Nose Ya

RIGHT

"Mommy, where do cupcakes come from?" "Well, when four gingerbread men fall in love, they buy houses next door to each other and when they really love one-another . . . a stork delivers them a cupcake."

FAR RIGHT

As the night goes on, feel free to get crazy and take this sweater off, as it can double as a board game.

Nice Cupcakes, Sweet

Tic Tacky Oh No

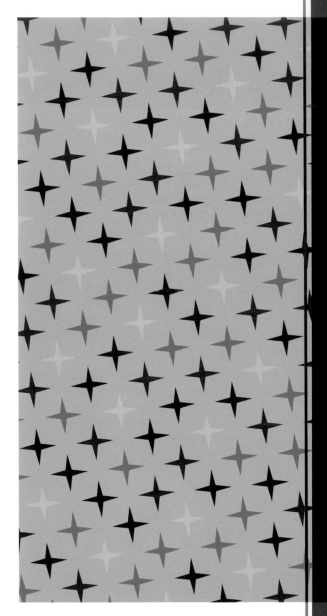

Is it even necessary for snowmen to wear mittens, hats, and scarves? They are made of snow, so the idea of keeping warm seems counterintuitive, right? Just look at the remnants of the melted departed. Sad. Why are they all smiling?

These flames are hot, and with the blend of wool, polyester, and synthetic fibers, the proud owner should check local fire hazard codes prior to wearing this in public.

The Vanishing

Burning Down the House

Leon once showed up to an Ugly Christmas Sweater Party wearing this and proclaimed with absolute confidence that he would win Ugliest Sweater, yelling, "Who else has an Ugly Sweater with their name on it, huh?!"

Dyslexic Leon

The whole gang shook their unopened gifts, trying to guess what was inside, but all they could hear was "Whah, whaah whaa . . . whaa-wha whaaha wha . . ."

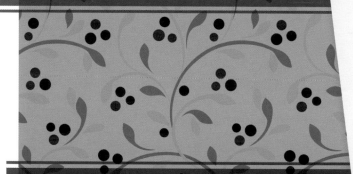

Peanut Exchange

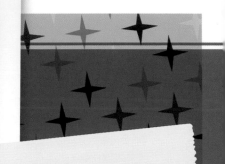

Pyramid Scheme

Mass Destruction

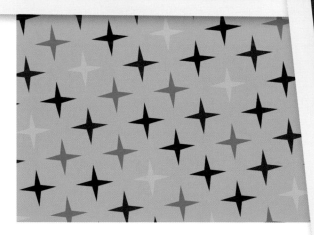

FAR LEFT

Snowmen need to make a living, too. You didn't think those corncob pipes filled themselves, did ya? Unfortunately, what snowmen have in heart they tend to lack in brains. This is a perfect example of a group that made a failed attempt at starting a pyramid scheme.

LEFT

Can anyone tell us what ever happened to the bus from the movie *Speed*? We think it just ran into this church.

It's my Pussy in a Box

ABOVE

This sweater depicts the *Kitten Saturday Night Live* version of Justin Timberlake and Andy Samberg's smash hit "Dick in a Box." Similarly to Timberlake, the kitten on the right has made so many cameo appearances on *Kitten SNL* that viewers are beginning to say, "Meowy meow meow," which translates to "Hey, what gives?"

RIGHT

These two pups fight for the attention of a prospective new family. Both know they would make a great gift on Christmas morning, and both know if they don't bring their "A" game they're even more likely to acquire kennel cough.

Party at the Pound

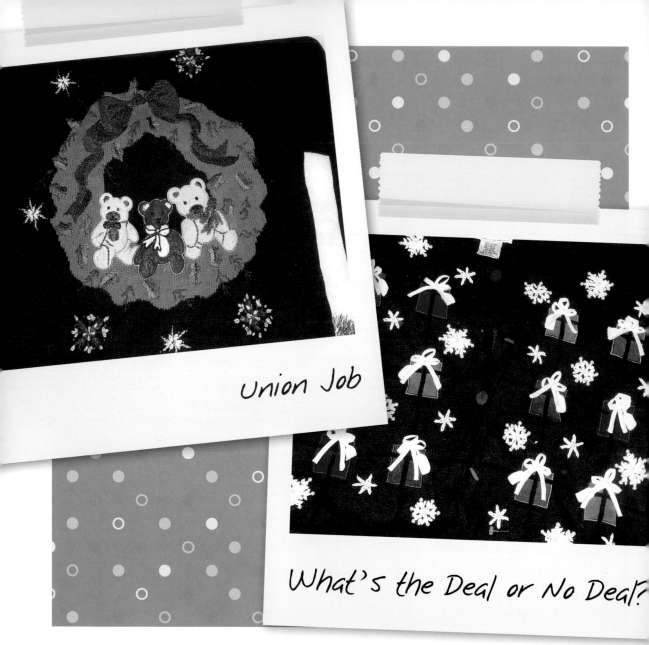

Union Job

What's the Deal or No Deal?

FAR LEFT

Members of the Local Bear 101 are seen here taking their seventh one-hour break during their eight-hour shift. Immediately following, the three bears will draw straws to determine who will tighten the red bow while the other two stand around and watch.

LEFT

Ever wonder what Christmas morning looks like at Howie Mandel's house? While the models are nowhere to be found, one thing is for sure: Howie's obsessive-compulsive disorder is in full effect as he's perfectly lined up the gifts, tied all of the bows identically and drenched each one individually with hand sanitizer.

When it comes to safety, Santa doesn't F around. Between his armed guards, armored high-speed train, and extremely smelly stockings, nobody is foolish enough to make an attempt at de-jollying Jolly St. Nick.

Santa is drafting his resignation letter once and for all. He wasn't sure whom to turn it in to, so he decided he would just post a status update to his Facebook account stating that he quits.

Santa's Secret Service

Santa Calls it Quits

Real Housedoes of Aspen

A Pair of Bears

FAR LEFT

Next season on Bravo: These deer love to ski and spend the big bucks. Tune in as Vixen starts the latest trend, red nose jobs . . . oh no she didn't!

LEFT

These bears love to compare the size of their candy canes.

Beary Gibb

Beary marches to the beat of his own drum, and that drum just happens to produce nothing but adult contemporary rock and classic disco hits. How deep is your love?

Everything must go! The gingerbread men have already been evicted from their gingerbread house, and it was recently reported that the Candy Shop was purchased by rapper 50 Cent, ironically for an estimated $0.50. 50 Cent invites everyone to come down to the Candy Shop and requests that you "don't stop until you hit the spot."

Candy Land Foreclosure

Supershort Stackers

The North Pole Dancer

FAR LEFT

Every winter, snowmen siblings Sam and Stan Stevens square off in a Secret Santa shopping spree. After sweeping through supermarkets for sugar, shoestrings, shampoo, and seersuckers, these showoffs start to do some serious stacking.

LEFT

Is that a candy cane in your belt, or are you just happy to see me? It's a well-known fact that Santa loves to keep the entire workshop entertained during the offseason.

As playful as these two felines may appear, do not be fooled. Scratchy McClaws and Whiskers "The Kid" Thompson are a modern-day Bonnie and Clyde. Close your doors, lock your windows, and place a saucer of milk in the middle of a busy road.

The Kittens That Stole Christmas

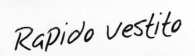

Rapido vestito

Crossing the border has never been easier; just disguise yourself and your family as snowmen. Who would ever question a pack of traveling snowmen?

RIGHT

In a desperate attempt to become our 51st state, the North Pole has begun the Americanization process. Snowmen are adorning themselves in the "red, white, and blue," Elves are downloading Toby Keith songs, and the reindeer were all laid off and are collecting unemployment.

FAR RIGHT

This sweater packs a powerful punch of Ugly. All the traditional yuletide symbols are represented on this monstrosity. You have wreaths, trees, candy canes, and presents. All that is missing are long lines full of impatient customers, massive credit card debt, and the disappointed look that kids get when they realize "Santa" is just Dad wandering around in his bathrobe haphazardly throwing presents under the tree.

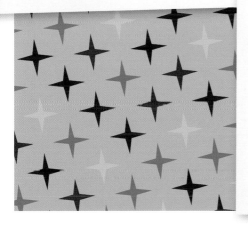

Freedom Frosty

Festive 'N' Fugly

BELOW

Everyone gets stressed around the holidays. Trying to find the right gift for everyone, finding time to make it to all the parties, and staying within your budget can make it seem like the world is on your shoulders. Whenever you are feeling down and your problems get the best of you, think of these four snowmen. Despite their temporary ailment, they have all managed to put a crooked smile on their crooked faces.

RIGHT

This snow dad worked the day shift at the graveyard and the graveyard shift at the Days Inn just to provide Christmas presents for his snow kids. Let's hope his snow wife remembers this when he comes home smelling like snow whiskey.

Jingle Bell's Palsy

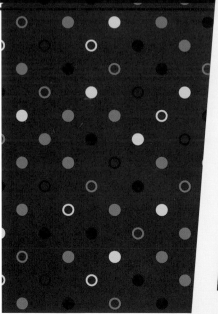

Dysfunctional Family

M. Light Shyamalan

Use your *Sixth Sense* to follow the *Signs* that lead to *The Happening* party next *Weekend at Bernie's.*

It's hard to tell from this sweater, but by the looks on their faces these boys are either innocently singing from a book of carols or checking out their first nudie mag that one stole from his older brother.

Choir Boys Will Be Boys

Holy Craft

This was just a boring sweatshirt of a bear holding a wreath before the puffy paint and glitter brought some excitement to it. We tried applying this practice to real-life, boring situations, but apparently judges frown on their jurors bringing puffy paint and glitter into their courtrooms.

Everyone knows that the penguin is a flightless bird. What everyone didn't know until this sweater was made was that during the time spent bound to the earth, they taught themselves the graceful art of figure skating. Now if they could only teach themselves how to sew flashy unitards . . .

Penguin Capades

Collar at your Boy

We would like to assure you that no animals were harmed, in the making of this sweater's collar . . . except for a couple.

When your significant other decides to wear this on your date night, you're on your own. They don't make a tiny blue pill strong enough to help you out.

Holly No Wood

You know when you're at a concert and the band plugs in the name of the city or state they are playing in and the crowd goes nuts? That's what we are doing here. What's up, Indiana?!?!? Are you ready to read!?!?!

Some teacher found a creative way to use the overflowing contents of her preschool's lost-and-found box. If only she could find a use for all the boogers she scraped from underneath the desks.

Hoosier Daddy

Lost and Found

Truth or Dare Jenga Presents

This sequinsy sweater gave us another gift exchange idea. Stack presents up Jenga-style, and if the present you pull topples the pile you open It, do a dare, or tell the truth about any topic. Sounds fun . . . until you try it and have to hear about your mom's first time. Some things you can't unhear.

The makers of this sweater couldn't decide on a single theme. So they mixed the DNA of various Christmas symbols in a petri dish and this is what grew. Rumor has it human DNA found its way into the dish and an underdeveloped head grew on the back.

Vest Tube Sweater

This sweater depicts the shady portion of the North Pole. This is made obvious by the dilapidated houses sharing the very same telephone wire that elves hang their tiny shoes over.

North Pole Projects

E.T.T.

Proving once and for all that they are technologically more advanced than we humans, this alien spaceship disguised as a tree is seen sucking up people's presents. Every year on December 26, numerous alien encounters are reported as they can be seen returning the toaster ovens and beard trimmers they have no need for. The government has tried to keep this hush-hush.

Heart On for Christmas

North Pole Adoption Agency

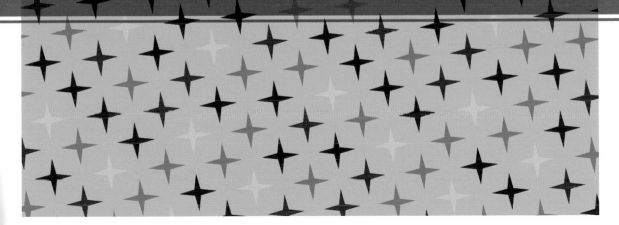

FAR LEFT

Wearing this sweater to your annual family gathering will let your loved ones know that you have your Christmas heart on.

LEFT

In a recent corporate takeover, Claus Enterprises acquired Stork Delivery Systems. Santa's duties have now expanded beyond giving presents to boys and girls to giving boys and girls as presents.

RIGHT

Oh what fun it is to wear, unless you want to get laid!

FAR RIGHT

This is where the most hardened Christmas convicts are locked up. They spend their time playing reindeer games for smokes, making license plates for sleighs, and fashioning shanks out of candy canes.

Celibacy Sweatshirt

Santa-tary Confinement

Snowmatch.com

Hot for Teacher

LEFT

Tired of the traditional dating scene, Frosty decided to search online for a soul mate. Frosty left disappointed because the tree looked much skinnier in its profile picture.

ABOVE

Ms. Johnson gave us the assignment to write an essay describing what we wanted for Christmas. "Perfect!" I thought to myself. "I can finally write down what I have been yearning for all year long!" Turns out Ms. Johnson also wanted the same thing for Christmas, but she will have to wait fifteen years (ten with good behavior) to get it again.

Santa cannot just run into the local gas station on Christmas Eve when he has to do his business. Unfortunately, someone has to take one for the team when the fat man needs to drop a Yule log.

Capitalizing on the early 1990s grunge scene, Santa spent much of the decade delivering gifts to the children of the world with a flannel gift sack. This went over much better than the disco-ball sack he used on Christmas Eve 1972, when fourteen Boeing 747s went down over the Pacific Ocean.

Santa's Porta-Potty

Santa's Got a Grungy Sack

Ornamental Disaster

Look at the Baby

FAR LEFT

Just because you *can* throw random ornaments on a sweater vest doesn't mean you *should*. If you actually put this on in the morning and said to yourself, "Yep, this reflects my personality," then we want to hang out with you.

LEFT

The best part of an Ugly Christmas Sweater Family Party is when you get to tell your cousin how ugly her kid really is.

Bears, much like dogs, sometimes latch on to inanimate objects and go to town. No one has ever known if they should stop them or just let them finish. When it comes to dogs, we say do whatever you feel is right, but when it comes to bears, we say let them do whatever they think feels good.

He'll Stop When He's Finished

The reindeer got sick of the fat man always yelling at them . . . so they decided to leave Santa to fend for himself. Last we heard, the reindeer all got gigs pulling carriages in downtown Chicago.

Hitchhiking Santa

I Love Holly Berry

Recipe for Disaster

FAR LEFT

Candy canes placed perfectly to form hearts, holly and berries, and little snowflakes placed in between them all. I know what you're thinking: "This is beautiful and full of Christmas cheer!" Not me. It makes me want to punch a bunny in the face.

LEFT

WARNING: Some of the ingredients have been listed multiple times to fill space. I mixed every ingredient together that was listed and put it in the oven for 15–18 minutes. A ten-foot-tall gingerbread man walked out of the oven and has taken over my house. He makes me sleep in the basement.

4th of December

ABOVE

Team Ugly is a firm supporter of the troops and the fine country they risk their lives for. What we are *not* firm supporters of is mixing two holidays together. You don't see families carving turkeys and eating stuffing while watching the Indy 500, do you? Wait. . . . The Indy 500 is a holiday . . . right?

RIGHT

You better "Think" about all the "Respect" you will get wearing this ugly sweater to your next "Party in the U.S.A."

Awreatha Franklin

WallPaper

Scarf Face

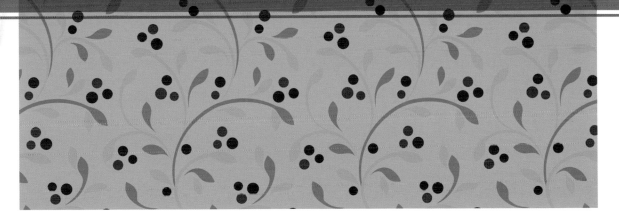

This is the perfect attire for those Ugly Christmas Sweater Parties held at dive bars. When that annoying friend of yours makes eye contact with you from across the bar, simply lean against the wall and blend right in!

Say 'ello to ma ugly friend! This sweater fled Cuba, where the warm climate rendered it useless. It came to the United States and made an infamous name for itself when the cocaine explosion hit in the 1980s. It is currently serving back-to-back life sentences in federal prison.

BELOW

If we answered our door to find this group standing outside, the last thing we would think was, "How adorable! Santa and some snowmen have come to spread Christmas cheer." It would be more like, "Call Will Smith! Earth has been invaded!"

RIGHT

At first glance, you may see a cheerful winter scene. If you look closer, you will see that the three snowmen in top hats are carrying guns wrapped in red-and-white tape and are robbing the poor lady of her presents. I hope they open the presents only to find blow-dryers. Those bastards.

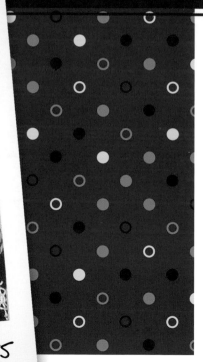

Creepy Christmas Carolers

Stick 'Em Up, Snowmen

Wreath Witherspoon

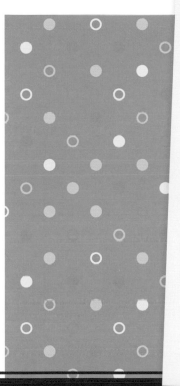

And the Three Bears

LEFT

At this point, you might as well go outside, take the giant wreath off of the front door, and just hang it around your neck. You're going to get just as many stupid looks, but at least with the wreath around your neck people will *know* you have mental issues instead of just wonder.

ABOVE

"My ice skates are way too small to support my morbidly obese body," says the first bear. "My skis are way too small for me after eating those five villagers yesterday," says the second bear. "When are those two fat asses going to learn to just follow my lead?" says the third bear.

Cup Check

Every Christmas Eve, these nutcrackers have been known to come to life at the stroke of midnight. These guys are not in search of the Rat King; they're looking to get down to business and crack some nuts. It is strongly recommended that the owner go to bed sporting a jock strap.

At first glance, this looks like a wonderful, snow-covered village. That's how he lures you in. Have you ever woken up to a snowman standing over you, breathing heavily while melting all over your leopard-print comforter? You don't want to know what it's like, trust me.

Psycho Snowman

Cat Scratch Fever

A couple different things may be going on here. One, the cat is stretching her adorable little paws as the old lady takes a break from her knitting to fetch the kitty a saucer of milk. Or two, the cats have eaten the old lady and taken over the pad for themselves. We're going with number two.

While Rudolph struggled to fit in at first, he has now taken the spotlight and garnered much of the attention. After a lot of infighting, Rudolph has decided to split off from the group and start a solo career, much like Peter Cetera did with Chicago.

Runaway Reindeer

NEAR

This sweater takes a look into the future of Christmas. Everyone knows that with Santa's horrible eating habits, and the fact that he only works one day a year, he won't be around forever. Therefore, reindeer will become bipeds so that they may sneak into your house and deliver the presents themselves.

FAR

From what we have heard, Prancer and Vixen found out that Dasher and Dancer haven't been actually doing any pulling for the past 134 years—they've kind of been just coasting along. Sources close to the story say Prancer has been on pulling enhancing drugs. Our money is on Prancer and Vixen.

merry Evolution

Reindeer Battle

Beam me up, Scottie

LEFT

The only thing worse than a little dog that yaps all day is a little dog that yaps all day while wearing clothes. Also, not a good idea to try to balance burning candles on the end of tree limbs.

RIGHT

Here's a safety tip, kids: Don't hang Bigfoot's socks over a raging fire that happens to be right next to a giant Christmas Tree. Is it me, or does it look like the sweater is actually starting to melt?

We Didn't Start the Fire

BELOW

Until we started slanging sweaters we had no idea that cardinals were a symbol of Christmas. We still aren't convinced, and think that sweater manufacturers are just lazy and need something red to fill space.

RIGHT

Just when you thought your days were short and nights were long, this guy shows up and makes everything feel better.

Old Man Winter Solstice

Cardinal Sin

Jacob's Cabin

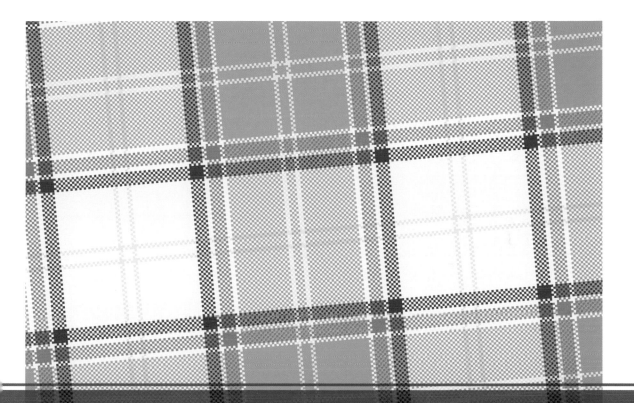

SPOILER ALERT: IF YOU HAVEN'T SEEN THE *LOST* FINALE YET, STOP READING!
A big Lostie Santa took a detour from his route over the Pacific and flew to the island to see for himself if Hurley was really the new protector of the island.

Team Ugly, out!!!

TEAM UGLY RECOMMENDS...

Every year, as the popularity of Ugly Christmas Sweater Parties grows, more and more people are throwing them. If you have read the preceding pages and feel that hosting a party of your own is impossible, then finding one to attend in your area shouldn't be. A quick online search will surely net you dozens of announcements for parties that are being held nearby. Although we would love to provide you with a comprehensive list of every party being held in North America, owing to the fragility of the world's ecosystems and the limited structural integrity of most bookshelves, we can highlight only a few of the most popular and longest-running parties.

Since 2001, the Commodore Ballroom has been packed with Ugly-Christmas-Sweater—wearing Vancouverites spreading ugly joy and raising money for the Union Gospel Missions drug recovery program. Toronto has held an annual Ugly Christmas Sweater Party and toy drive at Baby Huey's since 2004. Kansas City has held an Ugly Christmas Sweater Party yearly since 2005 to raise money for Operation Breakthrough, a local organization dedicated to helping children who live in poverty. Our fellow Hoosiers have been aiding Gleaners Food Bank since 2005 with Indy.com's Ugly Christmas Sweater Party in Indianapolis. Chicago and Minneapolis both host popular pub crawls that have sweater-clad patrons raising glasses in celebration and money for their local children's hospitals. Annual Ugly Christmas Sweater Parties in Boston and Los Angeles have been taking place since 2006, and both benefit local Boys & Girls Clubs. Wherever you live, you will no doubt be able to find a sweater soiree that is fun and benefits a worthy cause.

ABOUT TEAM UGLY

Team Ugly and UglyChristmasSweaterParty.com were founded by three good friends who love to have a great time. Adam, Brian, and Kevin met in the fall of 2000 while attending Indiana State University, and have spent the past decade making fun of one another, tricking one another to take on foolish bets, and generally monkeying around. They attended their first Ugly Christmas Sweater Party in 2006, and soon after were inspired to start a blog and online venture to bring Ugly Christmas Sweater Party joy to people all over the world.

Brian Miller. Odds are he came up with the idea for the party, but will show up late owing to the fact that he always waits until the last minute to get things done, and he's also convinced that it only takes ten minutes to get anywhere . . . no matter what. Brian's Ugly Christmas Sweater Party attire tends to cross genres, mixing a vintage candy cane vest, say, with a modern twist of lights or a tie that plays Christmas carols. His life ambition is to go back in time via a 1982 DeLorean DMC-12.

Adam Paulson. He can be found at the epicenter of any good party and has the ability to spread the word of a get-together faster than (insert a description that is the opposite of the Pony Express here). Adam's Ugly Christmas Sweater Party attire is often head to toe, and he's been known to sport a festive red fedora to the finer galas. His drink of choice is an ice-cold beer, and you best get out of his way should a tray of summer sausage and cheese appear.

Kevin Wool. Likely to be the first to show and last to leave, Kevin knows that the quality of a good party relies heavily on the setup and that the true fun isn't until the after-party. His Ugly Christmas Sweater Party attire is classic and timeless: a turtleneck and button-down vest, topped off with a plaid sport coat. Kevin would be perfectly content if he spent the rest of his life as a film critic by day and a steakhouse aficionado by night.

Visit Team Ugly at www.UglyChristmasSweaterParty.com